South to the Rio Grande

poems
Peter Hoheisel

Poems by Peter Hoheisel
Clare Songbirds Publishing House Poetry Series
ISBN 978-1-947653-80-1
Clare Songbirds Publishing House
South to the Rio Grande © 2019 Peter Hoheisel

All Rights Reserved. Clare Songbirds Publishing House retains right to reprint.
Permission to reprint individual poems must be obtained from the author who owns the copyright.

Printed in the United States of America
FIRST EDITION

Clare Songbirds Publishing House Mission Statement:
Clare Songbirds Publishing House was established to provide a print forum for the creation of limited edition, fine art from poets and writers, both established and emerging. We strive to reignite and continue a tradition of quality, accessible literary arts to the national and international community of writers, and readers. Chapbook manuscripts are carefully chosen for their ability to propel the expansion of art and ideas in literary form. We provide an accessible way to promote the art of words in order to resonate with, and impact, readers not yet familiar with the siren song of poets and writers. Clare Songbirds Publishing House espouses a singular cultural development where poetry creates community and becomes commonplace in public places.

140 Cottage Street
Auburn, New York 13021
www.claresongbirdspub.com

Contents

Getting There

Travelling Down to Texas: Middle Aged Fantasy	10
Approaching Texas	13
Driving Down to Texas	14
Good Advice	15
Plain Things Sing	16
Towards Lake Conroe	17
Missing Her	18
Fish Need Fresh Water	19
For Jane, Arriving	20
Freedom	21
Going to the Writer's Conference	22
Reincarnation	23
It's All Moved By Love	24
Do the Day	25
At the Turning of the Year	26
Bone Tired	27
Love Is	28
Wild Fish	29
Beyond Rapture	31
Camping at Broken Bow Lake, Oklahoma	33

Exploring

Sunrise at Mount Selman	36
At Old Fort Parker	37
Travelling to Laredo	38
At Houston, On the Coast	39
An Old Couple Selling Vegetables	40
Fishing at the Crystal Bar, Alpine, TX	41
Spring Break at Port Aransas	42
An Old Lady Hunting Treasure	44
Letting Go the School Year	45
Shall I Sing of A Summer's Day?	46
Art Teacher	47
Travelling to Canyon Lake	48
At Kerby Lane Coffee Shop With Her	49
Buzzard	50
Edge of the Wild	51
After the Day At Reynosa Market	52
Loss Creates Recognition	55

Being There

Jacksonville: Where Is It?	58
My Cadillac Existence	60
Sunset at Tyler, Texas	61
After Reading at Sul Ross University	62
Last Class of the Semester	63
At the End of the Semester	64
Favorite Time of the Year	65
At Spring Break	66
Christmas Vacation Begins at College	67
East Texas Men At the Faculty Meeting	68
The Four Stages of Life for Men in East Texas	69
Let Go the Toads	70
Ocotillo Plant: A Meditation	71
A Whole New Attitude	72
Sunday Morning Walk in Tyler, Texas	73
Sunshine on Pine Needles	75
A Stray in Uncertain February	76
For George Washington Hunt	78
A Prayer for My Frazzled Landlady	80
After Arguing With Her	81
November 1, All Saint's Day	82
Meditation on Sunday Morning	83
Portrait of a Morning	84
He's Gone	85
In Praise of Trees	86
Making Love to the Body of the World	87
Elegy for Montgomery Cowdry at Wilderways, Mount Selman, Texas	88
Coping With Change	91
As the Year Ends	92
At My Cabin	93
Deep in January	94
Jane on the Telephone	95
Unplanned Destination: An Elegy for the Columbia	96
An Elegy for Horace Edison	102
An Ordinary Sunday Morning	103
The Eyes of the Mockingbird	104
Alone	105

Thanks to Christopher Winn for his editorial services and encouragement. Thanks to Mark Hoheisel—my nephew—for suggesting the title.

Some poems in this book have appeared in the following publications:

The Langdon Review: Unplanned Destination
Hurakan: After the Day at Reynosa Market, Mexico
New Texas: Ocotillo Plant: A Meditation
Wild Cat: At Houston, On the Coast
The New Laurel Review: Fishing at the Crystal Bar, Alpine, Tx
Louisville Review: Spring Break at Port Aransas
The Hungry Chimera: A Prayer for My Frazzled Landlady
County Line: An Old Couple Selling Vegetables; Sunday Morning Walk in Tyler, Texas
Reunion: The Dallas Review: An Old Lady Hunting Treasure
Riverfeet Press: Edge of the Wild

Introduction

After finishing a three-year contract as poet-in-residence at Lake Linden High school in the Upper Peninsula of Michigan, in 1989, I moved to Tyler, Texas, to work with local schools integrating poetry and visual art, under the sponsorship of the Tyler Museum of Art.

Driving down from Michigan, stuck behind a slow-moving truck, packed to the brim with logs, about 100 miles from Tyler, I thought, "This could be Northern Michigan, with the hills and lakes and the logging of pine trees."

With one obvious difference. Climate. During summer in Texas, people huddle indoors with their air-conditioner humming, whereas in Michigan, one is outdoors as much as possible, enjoying the long, cool days which begin about 5:00 AM, and end gracefully in long, lingering sunsets about 10:00 PM. Residents of Upper Michigan know that the Snow Queen takes over in early November and reigns until the end of April. They know that the interminable dark days of winter are coming, when children leave for school before sunrise, and return to their warm, cozy homes after sunset.

After my year-long residency at the Tyler Art Museum, tired of the gypsy life of the wandering poet, the pampered and secure life in academia, which I had abandoned about twenty-five years before, called out to me with its seductive song.

Finding a temporary appointment as a lecturer at Sul Ross University in Alpine, Texas, I learned to appreciate the dry, desert climate of West Texas, the very opposite from the other side of the state, with its abundance of lakes, trees, and vegetation. We Scorpios love contrast and clear definition. Grey does not appeal to us. And so, I was blessed to experience two starkly different regions in one state.

After my year at Sul Ross University, a permanent job teaching Creative Writing, English, and Philosophy became available at Lon Morris College, in Jacksonville, Texas. Since then, Texas has been my home.

My first book, <u>North to Superior</u>, tries to portray the spirit of that magnificent part of Michigan near the shores of that greatest of the Great Lakes, a testament to the veracity of my home state's motto: Si Quaeris Amoenam Peninsulam, Circumspice. <u>South to the Rio Grande</u> likewise attempts to give the reader a feel for what it is like to live in my adopted state, whose people also live true to their motto: friendship.

Getting There

Travelling Down to Texas: Middle Aged Fantasy

1.

Down from Lake Superior and across Wisconsin
to Interstate thirty-five,
which twists and turns through the heart of Minneapolis
before it lances
through the center of the country
south to the Rio Grande.

I have driven through the heartland of the nation.
rolling toward the bottom of Arkansas.
Outside a neon-lit truck stop
on the way to Fayetteville,
at least a hundred miles away
jagged lightening splits the darkness
like some deity
forcing its will onto parched earth.

In my heavy blue Oldsmobile
I shatter space and time, and outdistance age.
Weighted with iron, this politically incorrect car
is fueled with power
sucked from the earth of the state which is my destination.

While my stepson
does push-ups at Fort Leonard Wood,
getting ready to fight
for the fuel which made our empire possible,
this steed
incarnates a wizardry
more dazzling
than anything a Roman Emperor
could have commanded to cross the lands he controlled.

2.

It is no longer fashionable,
as it was in Roman times to just take what you want.
Now our troops stand in the dust and the heat
and wait for permission from the United Nations.
This is the time of committee approval, of public opinion,

flattening
the spirit into quantity and mass
making everybody alike.
I am sick to death of people driving
small cars because it is ecologically sound.
The big boats of the fifties
sing in my blood;
thank God I am travelling to Tyler,
not Austin,
where everybody is so liberal and so correct and so tight.
Tyler has solid blood and guts religion.
Sin is real there,
liquor stores are banished to the next county,
and ladies who dye their hair with blue,
drive cars made by General Motors, not Japanese.

In this big car at eighty miles an hour
I indulge an ancient lust
more powerful in men perhaps
than even the vain desire to dominate women:
to annihilate space,
to force our way
across the land just to see what is there.

3.

Old folks travel a great deal these days,
follow Eliot's dictum that
old men should be explorers,
proving that the lust of the eye,
has more staying power than the phallus of the flesh.
And so chastity and faithfulness to one woman
come easier with time
as does at least a semblance of rational control.

All addictions seem to cool with age,
but I still, when I am seventy,
would like to be on a beach in Mexico
drinking Margaritas and Cuban cigars
served by lovely senoritas of the south.

God certainly has a sense of humor:
when we are able to make more seasoned choices

about the bodies with whom we join our throbbing flesh,
and when finally perhaps we are able to afford generation,
he lessens the desire.

And so now, a new adventure lures me down to Texas:
Divorced, all debts paid,
a new job in a new state,
owner of two houses and money in the bank,
inflamed with lust for travel
I will see,
if I can get drunk on the spirit of joy.

Approaching Texas

It's a moist, wet morning, warm in the
Ozarks:
Alma, Arkansas, where 3000 souls reside.

I slept on a mountaintop
curled up in the front seat of the car
like a cat
and woke to feel gentle warm rain
falling on my face through the open window.

What is in a half-century of life?
A greediness to stay alive.
Thoughts about health, security,
love's failures and success,
and a lust to do something new
after fifteen years of responsibility for others.
That occasional twinge in your hand
where a pin stitches bones together
from the football injury
when you decided
you did not want to crash against your fellow human beings.
And that joy in sheer movement,
seeing new things,
the desire to experience all there is in this world of illusion.

Driving Down to Texas

Near Broken Bow, Oklahoma
the shadows are lengthening and evening is coming in.
A warm wind gushes across the fields
and through the car, massaging us
with Southern fragrance.
We are in Northeast Texas & it is full summer again.
The wide fields are ripening
in the open space of my life.

Good Advice

At three fifteen, twenty-two miles from
Gilmer, Texas
with light rain coming down
a sign on a church:

God is able.
Are you willing?

What! Leave those
delicious resentments
proving that I am right and
She is wrong. Never, never, never.
It is so fine to be trapped in the
Past.
Resentment is wine to the ego
pleasant pain, proof that my definition of myself is real.

I pass two logging trucks
full of red pine, just like at my former home, in the north
and there's a shabby motel at Lake of the Pines.

At Gilmer,
a thunderstorm pours down in warm sheets.
Why do I avoid it?
Why can't I revel in the wetness like a
Child playing in the street?
Because I am adult,
addicted to images of past and future,
and my knowledge of what is good for me.

It's thirty-five miles to Tyler, and I am
high on fatigue and Diet Coke.
Crazy beings, we weep for what was not,
because we think we know what could have been.

Plain Things Sing

Past Buffalo,
on the way to Austin,
three gnarled and twisted trees
frame that pond
ablaze in sunshine and wind,
while a solitary horse stands in the field.

Redbud trees in the far distance
All blooming and shaking and showing off
lavender
in the spring wind,
sing
that the world
is filled with plain things
and that the act of existence is sheer wonder.

Those grey rocks,
which punctuate the hillside
with no reason for being anything other than
what they are,
create no questions and provide
no answers,
but simply glow
with the intense light of themselves.

Toward Lake Conroe

South past Lake Palestine
a blue heron
stands on the guardrail
taking his position with regard to
the morning sun rising fresh around him.
he stands out, outlined,
in the world of memory and context,
which teaches us what to see.

His intent is clear.
He lives in the now.
He wants a fish. He does not wallow in the world of
symbol and sign as I do.
What am I fishing for in all this travel?

Missing Her
With thanks to Andrew Marvell's *Coy Mistress*

Why not be wild
do something out of character,
leap over the mental walls
you have patiently created,
brick after fearful brick?

Drive 400 miles
just to see me because you are
horny
and demand that I satisfy you in your
body.

Forget all those spiritual rules
forget about being a nice girl.
Who wants that on her epitaph?
SHE WAS A GOOD GIRL.
You never have been one anyway.

A cat in heat stalks
paces and pads her leonine self across
the curve of the world
and does not worry about returning
to the place which she left.

Let your hair grow long so I can
drag you into my cave.

Ride in a canoe down a wild river
for ten days
rejoicing your body with the real world.

Hunt for wild things to eat.

Pull my pants down and
Demand I fill you with my warmth.

Fish Need Fresh Water

At the university,
the fountain is shut off for the winter.
Each time I pass it,
I notice the fish are still
when the water is not flowing.
They lay like slabs of wood,
cautious, breathing, observing-
just like people,
they need fresh water flowing,
to be lively, active.
My mind too is stale and still
moves with habitual perceptions.
What water
do I need in this desert area?

For Jane, Arriving

Silver shining through the dark,
night sky,
the airplane bearing you,
Lands
and there is nearness again--
that leap of the heart still
Real,
even though lines of living
have etched themselves into
our faces.
And,
older now, perhaps we are
Innocent enough to give ourselves
spaces
to be with one another
playing among
the wild flowers which we call the world.

Freedom

When there is space between men
there is freedom,
to associate with intent and longing
the thriving of all,
the depth of meaning in
neighbor.

Witness the difference between
cruising the roads of Upper Michigan
watching the world unfold
with no interference,
and being jammed
on a freeway in Austin, Texas
in late afternoon.

And when there is space a man
dominates time, and is not
ruled by it,
for freedom is defined as the
space in which to live and
the mastering of time within it.

Going to the Writers' Conference

We had driven through the first
arctic touch of winter slush and snow
with ice caked on the hood of the car
as we felt our way to central Texas,
one turn of the tire at a time,
sensitive to any change
in the security and surface of the road.

At San Marcos the bushes and trees encased in ice
shells
were dripping now and brilliant in the sun.

I thought of Frost's poem
about how ice had formed on the bare limbs of trees
in the night
how they melted and cracked
in an avalanche of diamond brilliance
with the touch of the warming sun in late morning.

We talked on that journey,
hoping to create understanding
so that any build up, of ice around the heart,
might melt and flow into living water
fresh enough to satisfy each other's thirst.

Reincarnation

We skim into the world
already humming with
decisiveness and fixed
ways of doing things.

Those fresh perspectives
over which we have been
mulling and ruminating in
uncluttered air, is now
pushed into bonds of feeling,
rigid rails of habit and the meshing
of thousands of ways of seeing things,
with what actually is.

We parachute in,
Forget what we have left,
take root for a time like a dandelion seed,
which bursts in a golden
statement from the earth
and under the sun, at just the right time.

"It's All Moved By Love"
Mandelstam

Yes.
Even fear,
because some desired condition
is threatened
and we are afraid to lose
what we love.

Our curse is
that we often love the lesser,
the paltry reflection
rather than the fulness
because for ourselves we want too little.

The half sight,
the trembling reach
the self-doubt because of
what our mothers told us.

All those illusions need chastening
because we believe we are undeserved
and need to be shocked into
the knowing that we are Sons of God.

Do the Day

Like a servant, time brings
in on a shining platter,
each one, each day
unshaped in absolute uniqueness.

The drear, the drudge, the film
of habit which coats our minds
obscures this truth, and truly

Some will endure this day
in suffering. May God
send them, rays of light,
lightness, a lightening which
separates them from their pain.

While I, so blessed, can move,
can think, can do, give
who and what I am
truly
to this day, today.

Light creeps in on this grey,
January day but that lazy sun a few months
hence, will be a
fierce force
igniting the sluggish earth
hot and demanding,
while for now, even in the grey, the grey

I can truly do the day, this day, today.

At the Turning of the Year

A couple of days after winter
solstice,
darkness still floods in,
its momentum unchecked
by a date on a calendar;
it takes awhile,
days, a few weeks,
for the turning to be evident:
a large ship moving
through deep waters,
can reverse direction only gradually.

The new year,
yet another paring down:
separating myself
from what now will never be.

What remains:
a daughter, fifteen,
with whose shyness and
coltish reticence I am
travelling across the face of Texas,
feeling its landscape
with the finger of our senses.

I have a job, which is ever
changing, and yet the same,
with new ways of being in it.

And I have a cup,
a blue mug,
Christmas gift from that daughter-
clean, circular,
shining in its completeness:
one gift, one daughter, one job, a new year ahead.

Bone Tired

Trapped in the tide of
weariness which creeps along the bone,
the blood sluggish
as the day drags itself into being
with the world defining itself again
apart from my consent.

Still the alarm.
Up and out.
Get vertical.
and get to whatever
and wherever that whatever is,
after coffee and a shower.

Deliberately dressing yourself,
one item of clothing at a time,
will get you through this disparate day,
this day of the slow and barely beating blood,
the weariness which creeps along the bone.

Love Is

as the poet says
sometimes hard
because we base our worth on getting it.

When it goes
think of a star-crazed coyote
singing sweetly across a crust of snow
on a February night.

How pure, how free, how chaste he is.

Wild Fish

Driving across Texas again,
your native state,
I feel my loss of you, your light in my life,
and an image from our courtship
comes back unannounced:
At the crystal-clear waterfall
in the hidden garden outside of Munising,
in Michigan,
feeding those fat trout
which rolled and boiled the
surface of the water in a flash of color,
sucking in the pellets
we bought from a dispenser
for twenty-five cents.

Tame, domestic fish
used to a life of ease
with nothing to do
but scoop up the love and care
dropped to them
by tourists, whenever they appeared.

With us it was different-
wild fish emerged from
the deep water within us,
large ones who with no pity
devoured with their sharp teeth
the us that we were trying to build.

Beyond Rapture

All my life I have hungered to be wanted
To arrive, to be there, breathing and stable
Immersed in a particular world with commitment.

That pink explosion of flowers
At the tips of the bush outside my window,
Sways gently in the East Texas breeze,
And whispers to my soul, murmurings of arrival.

Camping at Broken Bow Lake, Oklahoma

1

A light wind furrows the face of the lake.
A pale sun casts a silver band
Across the greenish,
Grey water.
I walk along the shore.

Yesterday I found a chunk of crystal:
This trip's souvenir.

A Monarch butterfly greeted me in the morning
Down by the lake washing,
He seemed to say "Welcome to this beautiful day."

2

I walk along the trail as the misty morning
Ripens into consciousness
And a feathery spider web brushes my face.
It is good to stop.
How little we see, when we are in motion.

That spider web makes me notice
A drama unfolding above me.
Wheeling silently against the sky,
Are hundreds of my Monarch friends
Also stopping here to camp,
On their way to winter in Mexico.

Then I see one of them,
Caught in a web high up,
Suspended between clumps of pine needles.
All night, a spider,
Nocturnal fishermen, patiently set out his net strand by strand.
He, too, a tiny crouched figure is silhouetted
About a foot from the butterfly which
Flutters helplessly against the uncaring sky.
The more he struggles against the web,
The more he dooms himself.

Dozens of Monarchs wheel in the sky
Above the webs, above the trees; now that
I have stopped and become still,
I can actually hear the useless fluttering wings
Of the one who is trapped.

The butterfly seems a higher order of being.
He eats the flower, but does not kill it.
The spider kills, sucks life from the butterfly
Until only a hollow husk remains.
I leave saddened.
Deciding not to intervene,
Just because the spider is ugly
And the butterfly beautiful.

3

I am down now, from the north,
Far from the cold grey granite of the Huron Mountains by Lake Superior,
The oldest mountains in the world they say,
Resting here at Broken Bow Lake,
Like those other migrants, the butterflies.

The rocks are strands of shale interlaced with quartz.
The shale has a smooth, oily quality to it.
It splits when it shatters.
Is more vulnerable,
More open, than those rocks in the north.

I have worked to be here,
To have this space and time,
My gift to myself: to examine the categories
My mind has constructed.

This lake was not here once.
The islands which stretch before me as far as I can see
Were the tops of mountains.
Now cold, clean water, covers old configurations,
Creates new inhabitants, makes radical changes
Excites me with fresh possibilities for a new life.

Exploring

Sunrise at Mt. Selman

Fog layers gray, rest in
The spaces between the
Trees which stretch east
Towards Louisiana, the
Hills undulating across
The face of the land.

The rising sun reddens the
Strands of cloud across the
Blue face of the sky and then
Turns them gold creating
out of this ancient earth
Another new day, un-minted yet.

At Old Fort Parker

A weather-beaten stockade and
clay chimneys replicate that haven against Comanches.
On the road to it,
vultures took their ease at the top of a dead tree,
outlined against an azure sky.

The Commanches say a man
must dream,
(because a woman
has the children and they are her dream)
dream a vision from within
so his spirit can flow.

They took Cynthia Ann at nine years away from here;
those Comanches implanted
their spirit and seed in her so completely
that she made a son
so that when Sullivan Ross stole her back,
dragged her away from her people again, twice thwarting her will,
she died, soon after, with a broken heart,
separated from her dream, her tender creation, her son.

All of the actors
in this particular drama are
gone now.
What remains?
Vultures, the blue sky, and
the fort, through which we can wander at leisure.

Travelling to Laredo

Sprawled in the back of the suburban,
cruising through cactus and cattle country,
the ladies drive and chatter in the front,
consider giving the finger
to a Greyhound bus driver
who has rudely cut them off
and I think about how Whitman
loved the hum of the human voice.
Old Walt
would enjoy being chauffeured across Texas,
loafing at his ease,
at seventy-five miles an hour, & occasionally napping.

At Houston, On the Coast

At the underbelly of America,
it is night now and the salt stung air
flings itself across the raucous beach,
pounding waves against the shore.

Somewhere out there
Portugese men of war
float like mines, sent from the Middle East.
Fish breathe this oil-soaked, war-soaked air,
suck it into their gills,
just as we inevitably take
the wrong kind of women into our souls.

The beach of our imagination
searches for the kind of breast which suckled
us, and we surrender again, and again, and again,
to our mothers.

An Old Couple Selling Vegetables

I passed them twice,
Thundering down highway 175
In my shiny black van, thinking
Someday I have to stop and buy something.
They sat there, an old couple, as if
They had themselves grown out of the soil,
Selling vegetables from a rickety stand.

Fortune favored me this time
Because sometimes
One chance at something is all we get.
I did stop, that third time, and
Got onions, potatoes with the dirt
Still clinging to them, and tomatoes
So red you thought the rising sun
Had incarnated in them,
Which of course it had.

I picture them, year after year,
Rising in the cool of the morning
To tend the children they planted
With their own hands in springtime
So that pampered scholars like me
Can stop at the side of the road
And buy real food grown by real people who actually work.

Fishing at the Crystal Bar, Alpine, Tx

It's a clear night at the Crystal Bar,
they sway and cleave, fishing
for love while higher intellects
play dominoes and the lower thrust
their cues at pool balls hoping to
sink into a soft pocket, everybody
out to make points with the hoops of
their hair, roping some steer or heifer;

It's all ages here- grandmothers, as well as
those who are being weaned
and the middle-aged who
can be at home anywhere,
who know that where the feet are, is important,
not where the heart is.

And so we sway and weave as feeling
follows doing and at closing time,
everyone congregates outside the door
like a huge school of fish,
lest a keeper slip away into the lonely night.

Spring Break at Port Aransas

I.

The surf is roaring;
Strong wind.
Foam-flecked frothing, in
Flowing, attacking the shore.

No gentle pulse of ocean, here,
No quiet ebb and flow, but
Constant shore scouring.
Slashing, wave after wave,
Shredding old configurations.

Old thought patterns,
Thrown furled, uproared, aloft
Star-studded dissolution
Cleanses the mind.

II.

Feel full sun,
Early-spring cool wind,
Just Be Here.
Hear spring, see the break,
The breaking waves roar endlessly
Along the beach.

All Texas folk flock to the beach.
Bared and pared down to the briefs.
Amblers walk along the shore
Smoking, poking at shells,
All aimless idle gods;
Hairy pot-bellied males,
Young taut girls undraped, wrapped tight
In their skin, glowing,
Swimsuit swatches,
No unwanted furrow or fold,
Perfect, proud, in plain view,
Hiding in their bodies.

And old folks, thin flesh folding
Into itself, felled by life's
Falling, content in their shrinking.

Sea gulls,
Pelicans
Black birds,
All, all of us, idle gods
Awake to the sand,
To the sun
To hear the roaring, the roaring,
Of the waves
The incessant scouring of the shore.

An Old Lady Hunting Treasure

Not ready yet, for heavenly treasures,
each morning, she is out there
in front of the Sandy Shores Hotel
sweeping Corpus Christi beach
with her metal detector.

In a blue baseball cap
And plastic shoes,
The breeze flaps her
Print dress, outlining
Her slender body.

She is that age beyond
Age,
Is everything she is going to be.

I asked her what
Were the most
Exciting gifts
That her mesh basket
Had scooped from the sand:
"old silver coins, one was 1853.
And rings, one with rubies in it,
Lots of class rings."

Letting Go the School Year

In a canoe, floating down
the Brazos River,
below the dam at Possum Kingdom,
I will see the towering limestone cliffs,
as the river
snakes its way in wide loops
traveling to the Gulf of Mexico.
Clear, cold water.
A warm sun
beading up the sweat on my body.

Casting shining lures
into the dark, deep holes along the bank,
hunting trout and striped bass,
and float along in silence
and perhaps surprise a deer
which has come to the water's edge for a drink;
in evening, at the campsite,
the fish will broil slowly
in butter and lemon juice
wrapped in foil
and laid on a bed of coals
distilled from a wood fire.

At this time,
the events of the past year-
will pass me by
they are what they are for better
or worse,
because the world goes on,
oblivious to what I feel or think.

These times are precious:
when you have done all you can do
to accomplish your purpose;
when all that is
exists for your pleasure & contemplation,
and the only necessary response is praise.

Shall I Sing of a Summer's Day?

Waking up,
caressed into the day by light and birdsong
which slowly
filters into consciousness now,

Leaving those nightly excursions
to other planes of existence
beached again on the familiar shoreline
of this body

which I have worn now for quite some time
and with whom I have become familiar, and fond of
as our relationship has progressed over the years.

It asks now for
motion
fresh coffee and cold water,
modest requests,

filling the tank for clear sailing and remarkable adventure.

Art Teacher

Vivacious and energetic this Leo
prowls her art class speaking in complete sentences
molding those middle schoolers
like lumps of clay.
Exhorting, cajoling, praising, threatening
she ignites the fires of their minds
so that the spirit inside presses into
the things they make.

Travelling to Canyon Lake

The charcoal earth east of Taylor,
stretches to the horizon furrowed in all directions
under a December sun.
This cold spell in Texas
(an arrowhead from the Arctic)
pierced the land yesterday
dusting it with frost
so that the bushes around that blue pond outside of Marquez
looked as if some passing artist
had sketched just them,
leaving the blue water and yellow green leaves
high in that tree
at the edge of the water,
untouched, just for contrast.

At Kerby Lane Coffee Shop with Her

It is a kind of brimming,
a from within flowing,
a kind of loose tension,
as we caress our coffee cups.

Sitting across from one another at the café,
The cold porcelain boundaries us.
A cascade of words
flows from our spirits mingling,
as springtime brightness
creates rainbow light outside,
as we touch, and take,
and feast on the sacrament
of the coffee cups at the cafe, at Kerby Lane.

Buzzard

A natural in the air,
glider graceful,
playing with air currents
with an eye toward breakfast.

Perhaps an armadillo
nicely cooked in the oven
of the previous day's sun.

God's gift,
he keeps the world neat and recycles life.

Edge of the Wild

It happens suddenly. You are trolling
Steadily, in evening, with the sun sinking
Toward the rim of the world,
As the stars begin their bright appearance.

The sea swells, lifts and carries us
In steady rhythm, it dips and ascends
As we plow through the warm, wet Gulf of Mexico,

And, in an instant
The sea churns around you,
Slashings of water fret
The surface, with explosions.
There is a hissing of water and ferocity
As the wild, sinewy,
Silver mackerel, attack a school
Of bait fish, and
One of those feeders hammers my lure
And plunges heavy and deep,
And there is only the fish, and the
Sea, and the rhythm of his running, and your hauling,
And you will kill and eat him, or you will not
As the day descends into night.

This is aloneness:
At the edge of that utter wildness,
The ocean spreading empty and
Unfathomable for hundreds of miles
And thousands, millions, of living
Wild things, strange things,
And you dance for an instant
At the cusp of it
Far from cities and conceptual
Concerns, and you are one with these wild things,
At the edge of hundreds of miles of desolate ocean
And reality is condensed to
The running of the strong fish
Against the strength in your arms,
A single filament
Connecting his fierce kingdom to yours,
Which seems unreal in comparison.

After the Day at Reynosa Market, Mexico

1

After supper, I smoke a Delicado cigarette;
the red bright tip becomes ash,
distills the flavor of
sun-baked Mexican fields.
Jane cuts cloth quietly,
the scissors swishing through fabric
and Sylvia recites Gertrude Stein
pouring her musical words into the world.
Lobo waits on the porch
under the Texas stars.
Guards any flashes of affection
which come her way,
fends off other dogs
as the house descends to silence
under bright Orion
fixed certainly
in the dark canopy above which cradles us.

2

The moon rose early today.
We saw it coming up in the mid-afternoon
across the Rio Grande over in Raynosa,
where in the plaza we mounted painted horses
for pictures.
Choosing our stances in the world,
after watching
that red-frocked altar boy going about
his father's business in the domed church with its wide arches,
while in the market
chilies, beans, garlic, and pistachios overflowed their bins.

3

In the market, shops angled into shops,
corners stuffed with objects
waiting to be chosen and loved,
waiting to stand out in the world.
Strangers,
we were mazed into them,

flowed with the pull of things
unaware of when or where we would emerge.
The mass of things at the market condenses in my mind
to those delicate glass wishing wells in one of the stalls
symbols of the heart
which we take with us wherever we go.

4

A fresh pot of coffee gurgles over in the corner now.
All of us in this house
have learned the price of admission
and learned that it is simple:
you ask for what you want,
you grasp the handle on the door,
and step either in or out,
one step after another.
deciding you will lean into the dark,
embracing it as a friend and trusting signposts
which often are the simplest and most basic things:
a fragrant cigarette which tastes real and burns slowly,
or praying together before supper,
a sign that
no one of us here can claim competence or control.

5

Sylvia quoted an old Mexican saying,
"You dress up the monkey so that someone else can
dance with him," after she told Frank, her ex-husband,
how he has improved through her influence,
even though, while he now shares this house for a time,
he no longer shares her bed.
Yes, it is a good saying.
We have all danced with a number of monkeys,
and, dressed or undressed, made monkeys of ourselves
while we huddled
in various corners of self-accusation.

6

Mas, Mas, Mas
that one sign said in neon above a shop.
Gertrude Stein would love its non-specificity.

Who knows what that store sells?
Who cares?
That kind of sign will drag you in
for it perfectly defines
the condition of our human hearts.
Its promise is infinite, more advanced than a new advertisement
for a Japanese car which vulgarly tell us
what we are supposed to buy
even through no one has yet seen the vehicle.

But Mas, mas, mas- that is the perfect ad,
the perfect sign.
It could be a church or brothel,
the big breast of the world that says,
I am your Cornucopia.

7

Lobo, the stray who sits patiently outside the door,
would understand it perfectly.
She has had her fill of menos, menos, menos.
When you pet her, or feed her, she makes a low gurgling sound,
gulping in love,
patiently repeating over and over
mas, mas, mas.

Loss Creates Recognition

It is strange,
when you are stripped,
wrenched from a person
or condition upon which
you depended
how unreal the world seems.
No thing matters.

And then from
deep down,
a kind of electrical
charge, a power
which is filling,
is filling what?
It is something you had not
known
had been ignoring,
a being who
can stride across the world
and conquer it all
or simply let it go
and
vanish
in the gathering mist
where nothing appears as it is.

Being There

Jacksonville: Where Is It?

Jacksonville,
"a place to put down
Roots," says the sign as
you enter the town, and when
the Yankee arrived, it was, he thought,
a stop in the road, a pause,
a notch in the belt of a career,

Never dreaming that the sign
Was prophecy, that a house,
A cat, and a retirement plan
Would sink his roots into
The red soil
Like those famous
Tomatoes, pride of the town.

When he first explored
the streets of Jacksonville,
He asked "where is it?
Where exactly is the heart of town?"
A bank, and antique shop, and
A furniture store did not seem focus enough.

And so he roamed and wandered,
Street led to street,
A neat brick home might be
next to a shabby one
with a junk car in the yard,
and he found
where the upper-middle
class lives, and the old section, and
the black section, and where Hispanics
dwell and

he moved on still asking
"where is this town? What is the
spirit of this place?" and the Basket
factory said " I am Jacksonville"
and Tally Ho Plastic said
" I am Jacksonville," and

the Mexicans, full of hope, who wait on
the street behind Brookshires said "Here we are!
Here we are! Hire us, We also are Jacksonville."

The travelers from north to south
And south to north pass car dealers,
And Whataburger and Walmart
As they flit by on highway 69
And give not a second's thought to us,
But it is strange

how you can grow fond
Of such a modest place,
Such an earthy place, whose
Claim to fame is not finance,
or media, or exploration of space
but the humble
Tomato,

a place where roots
can grow silently in the night
nourished by the cool
and sweet rain of spring and winter
and you
wake one morning and realize,
"How strange, <u>this</u> is home."

A Cadillac Existence

I have a Cadillac existence,
wholly satisfactory and with gold trim.

Sixty-eight degrees of sunshine,
February fourth in Texas
deep in the heart of winter,
heading home for a nap
with a belly full of prime sirloin,
a regular check
which underwrites my present and future existence,
a good woman,
no dog,
three more child support payments,
and an old shiny car
which hums down the highway on cruise control,
parting this day into
distinct chapters, full of tenacity and purpose.

Sunset at Tyler, Texas

Like molten lava layered against the sky
clouds in flaming orange and pink and grey shades
flowing
across the face of a still blue sky
in front of the setting sun.

You want to hold it, to say,
Stop, just be there for me to look at
when I want to.
Painters can do that for us:
Indulge our lust to pin down beauty
and so we get married and take pictures
and make passionate war against change and death.

The shades deepen.
I stop my car and tell myself to just look,
soak up those blazing colors and let the traffic roll by me.
It grows darker now
and there is a sadness that there will never be another one
quite like this,
the way we feel after we make love.

It grows darker now.
The sun pulls down away from us,
like a mother sending its earth child to sleep,
calling the people of Tyler indoors,
and Venus, the evening star,
grows bright,
bringing us the children of night
who will show off for us,
 all night long
whether we notice them or not.

After Reading Papers at Sul Ross University

Out of the black void
of descending December darkness,
I emerge from the bowels of this building
where I have labored
since five a.m. on student compositions.

When I walked to work,
the stars were bright points of light
in the clear Southwest Texas sky.
We are star-stuff, made from them,
said the astronomer
at McDonald Observatory.
I don't feel like one, however.

The University was a tomb
at the early hour I arrived,
a black stillness lit only
with the fire and struggle
of getting words straight.

What does it all mean?
The sun-splashed world of early morning,
the clear mountains
holding the souls of Alpine in their eternal hands,
the birds chirping to the sun.
Nothing answers; everything simply is.

Last Class of the Semester

It is like that moment when a man in lust,
knows she will.

At the edge of ecstasy,
both inside and outside of it

alert to the wonders
which will be revealed

absolute freedom on the horizon,
to throw off the clothes we have been wearing

to hurl the mask of professor,
who needs to make something happen each day,

into the closet for a few months,
to run out the door and make love with the world.

At the End of the Semester

Soon, Stretch,
Ease into each day entirely
as caprice and desire dictate.

No more mastery of self:
Springing out of bed at 5:30 AM
in all seasons and conditions.
The almighty shower
Symbol of a new day.
Meeting with whole heart
all those classes, all those assignments.
Each day an island of order
knowing
it will all amount to a continent
of organization and clarity at semester's end.

Now, though,
it's almost over
except for the tallying tomorrow morning,
and turning grades in.

Nothing will fling itself onto my desk,
panting for love and attention;
it will return to a simple slab of wooden potency,
like the world the night before God spoke.

Favorite Time of Year

It's the top of May and we
are firmly in final examination week,
blessed quiet while students shape and express,
their knowing,
and I
organize their earnings for the semester
those columns of achievement or lack thereof.

The letters A to F march across my green record book,
reach a definite end, a blank space,
a square on the page where time and possibility have
ended,
run out for this class,
a death,
a severing of bonds and a
final accounting of the quality of our relationship,
from my point of view.

At Spring Break

Nothing need be done:
mid-term grades are in
and by now my students
and I have firmly fixed
ideas about one another.

The eager ones—
On time every day
like ships on course,
masters of their fate,
giving themselves,
growing powers of thought and observation;
in contrast to the slackers who
come to class with no books
or paper, when they are so moved,
and
immediately slouch down,
as if I had forced them to be there.

All gone now, we are freed
From the images of one another
for a week or so.
I congeal into my native self,
slough off
my role and people's images
of me, am hanging out in a nice
hotel in a suite high up
staring out at bare fields,
seated at a plain table,
with nothing in particular to do.

Christmas Vacation Begins at the College

Silence descends upon the dormitory.
Young undefined energy
is dispersed to wider spaces,
and the building relaxes,
doesn't have to preserve any images.
Bricks become mere bricks again
and doors go in or out
without doubt or meaning,
the way the world was when it was new.

East Texas Men at the Faculty Meeting

Magnificent and stone-faced they sit,
The men,
Grey-haired victors in life's testing,
While the women, like governments,
Yammer and jabber, lacerate air with their
Fertile wills;
Silent, beyond taxation and self-contained
The men observe,
Hold their own inner counsel,
Think about the cigars they will fire up
When the meeting is over,
Clearing the atmosphere with fragrant and healing smoke.

The Four Stages of Life for Men in Northeast Texas
(with thanks to Shakespeare)

The First

Boundless male company, cool, permissive,
Cruising back roads in pick ups,
Pop frosty foaming Coors
Iced deep in the heart of the cooler.
Hurl the empties out the window, shining,
Adornment for the roadway,
Freedom and virility expressing itself.

The Second

Compromise occurs,
One particular woman, fewer friends.
A trip to the preacher, before a child springs forth,
squalling, dependent.
A steady job, an incipient belly,
He roots himself in earth.

The Third

In- laws, mortgage, thankless children and
Regular church, punctuated by glorious moments
At deer camp,
endless poker playing, amid beer bravery,
evokes the vigor of youth, long into the starry night,
as the belly attains maximum girth.

The Fourth and Final Stage

In the rocker, coffee on the porch
growing into silence.
He awaits the first of the month social security check.
Words from the wife
Are mockingbirds
Fussing in branches,
A melody,
The music of God,
while sunrise streams in great shafts of light hurled
like beckoning angels, across the sky.

Let Go the Toads

It's finally Spring, and
The sun asserts itself
In a strong comeback
From its Southern
Vacation in Mexico.

Sweet young leaves
Shine and shimmer,
Warm the roots which feed their dance.

I, too, nourish myself with the shape of things within me,
Manage them or pass them by,
Cherishing no image from the past.
Winter is over. It is time for the new. Now.

In the back yard, at the pool,
Toads croak their throbbing love songs
Into the night,
Woo one another in moisture-laden,
Moon-soaked air.
The clamor of this yearly ritual
Mildly interests the cat,
But is too fastidious and self-contained
To care deeply about them,
their slimy smells and strange sounds.

Learn from the cat.
Notice the toads in your life, but pass them by.
Let them croak freely and mate with fellow toads.

Ocotillo Plant: A Meditation on Roots

Slender branches reach to sky
pushing from a solid bunched base.
Oblivious to the way others bend,
they rise to the sun
each branch boisterous in its own shape.

You don't see their thorns
until you get
close to them
like the defenses we erect
Against those who can touch us.

Like wild men buried in the dirt
pushing their spiked heads up
they grow in community,
but not too close to one another,
as if they know
that moisture is scarce
and that growing things need space.

It is easier, to be single,
rather than a cracked and crazed union
abrading against one another's barricades
erected long ago
against those towering beings
who ordered us around
when they were in wild disorder themselves.

A Whole New Attitude

At fifty-five,
he is still able
to hit a hardball, and
in his last game he went two for three.
The other time he struck out
with three straight swings.

He is a new kind of player now,
different from the way he was in college
when he would watch each ball carefully,
assessing its position in the strike zone.

Now he takes charge.
Is up at the plate
to hit the ball,
not watch it fly by,
and so he swings at anything
he can lay the bat on,
and wishes some coach
had told him to swing at whatever
He could hit
when he was twenty-one.

Sunday Morning Walk in Tyler, Texas

Bird songs
and myself
early moving into the day,
gradually warming
with a hint of the September heat to come
in the somnolent air
moving
through this morning on Azalea Street,
while the rest of the world is wrapped in Sunday indolence.

A walker in the body
bringing all this singing world into himself,
and stopping
to touch the scent of some blooms on a bush,
and his soul shouting:
"I am here,"
"Now."
"I am."
"Everything is."

Sunshine on the Pine Needles

The sun,
kisses the pine needles moving slowly in the breeze,
splashes them lavishly in constant giving
framed against the barky backdrop of the red pines rooted
in the orange earth of East Texas dirt.
A light wind moves them.

We also move our selves within this scene
growing straight from the earth,
sometimes bending, and, yes
at times, bold against the wind,
rooted in all that has made us what we are.

The wind moves against the pine needles
and they respond,
while the sun caresses their surfaces
the way a man's hand moves over the body of his beloved
so that every soft space is touched.

Light enables us,
in- ables us, to caress surfaces
make love with them while we breathe,
in- tense contact,
until light and life
expressed in discreet particulars,
partial, yet substantive, moving and unmoved in one being,
our selves, all embraced in I Am and It Is.

Light each day
Reveals new possibilities
We shower, have coffee, shave.
It all seems the same.
Yet, this very day, we will see
new angles and planes, enlightened surfaces, shadowy crevices,
fresh perspectives will sing
to the sweet organization which is us, at this time, in this moment.

A Stray in Uncertain February

That stray black dog,
her tail a curved apostrophe,
pointing to the sky,
flits around campus.

Perhaps some Labrador in her,
she's frisky and obviously without a home,
unattached, fur, skin and bones.

She lets no one approach her;
some students give her food,
but the giver must
back off, before she will eat.

Is she perhaps beyond entering
back into the comfort of domesticity?
Is a certain and definite home and
regular meals and a territory to guard
a possibility
which wandering has leached
from her soul?

Some dogs, like humans,
go wild and a
relationship of trust is a
distant memory, if it ever was.

A new spring is
on its way,
and
the shape of this growing season
has yet to be determined.

Will my newly planted plum trees
Blossom?

Still cold are earth and water,
but they are there brooding in
silence, and
something will grow
when it decides to.

Like that skittish, black stray,
the edge of the wild, the unpredictable
is always out there,
and what is real will come to us
in its own good time.

For George Washington Hunt
1938-2013

It was near Christmas,
In one of the coldest winters

When he moved on,
George Hunt,
Ever committed
To the light which
Infused his soul.

So difficult in our
Culture which worships the grey
And indistinct,
And is ever ready to take offence,
To understand a man
Whose convictions and actual life formed an indivisible union.

So hard to understand a man
Who gave everything to whatever he did.
A man who,
From his abundance,
Gave to those
Many would deem undeserving.

What remains is his
Living testament that, no matter what
Wounds inflict, inhabit
Our souls
No matter how imperfect
The conditions which nurtured us,
We can create abundance for our children,
And for many
Whose names we shall never know.

What remains are all those
Living souls
Whom he has touched
With his giving
With his laughter
And with his smiles.

And so, Buzz,
By giving from
What you had honestly earned,
Your Testament shines:
The Universe is Fullness,
Giving is its Essence.
And since you
Were One with It,
You now,
As the Indians say,
Walk among the stars,
Laugh with the angels,
And
Explore the infinite universe,
At home
In large new worlds.

A Prayer for My Frazzled Landlady

Fresh coffee, first cup
from the pot, which is always the best,
and squares of sunlight splashing on
my legs as I lounge on the
cool print couch in morning,
reading a Victorian novel,
filled with unhurried words
and drawing rooms, whatever those are.

Ritual abounds in that world
where the eternal enfolds the present,
and the press of the mundane, is managed by others.

I wish that you too could taste
the joy of what it means to live from within yourself
instead of feeding on the agonies of others,
the battered down bruised souls who constantly claim yours.
They always, always, always have a good reason.

You would have enjoyed that vanished world of long ago
when there was space and time and manners, and,
most of all, ceremony and silence, which enables
The presence of grace;
a world in which cigars are smoked,
tea is served, and sherry is sipped for its own sweet sake.

After Arguing with Her

Lights across Lake Palestine
flicker in the darkness.
Points of light and heat emerged
as our shadows grappled.
with one another during that last
time together.

Confession did not take away our sins.
We kept
freshly experiencing them, and
since we do not deserve love
the cherished image of ourselves remains secure.

So we are alone in our lashing out,
our meagre defense against the thrashings
we received when we were tender;
and it is good that we learn to hate one another.
It is more amenable to control.
Love weakens us, makes us vulnerable,
makes our opinions,
suspicious, makes us, possibly,
horror of horrors, wrong.

November I, All Saint's Day

It's serious exfoliating time,
As the world reveals its structure
And outline,

Trees bare love bonny
Inside bringing, bringing in
The boisterous green banished into
Lean longing and enfolding.

In love. I am in Love, flowing
Forth, fathering my life into a
Certain solidity.

No longer wanting waking, but
Awake, while the world grows lean and visible.

Meditation on Sunday Morning

1

The church rings its hollow bell
at the Sunday morning city
shouting "thou shalt not"
and the men and women stretch,
decide to sleep in,
make languorous love
search for strength from within:
a tender word,
that time on the beach in the sun
with the waves swishing
possessing one another
because each had a self to be possessed.

2

Thou shall,
says the silence.
If it takes days, months, years, centuries,
thou shall,
forge thyself with fierce patience
and face the mornings of possibilities
with flinty, flashing eyes.

3

Then after the omnipotence of sleep,
the drama of dreams
face that day's dawn
with a chisel in one hand
a hammer in the other, waiting for it to Speak.

Portrait of a Morning

The year young in tender leaf and
planting in the soil beds
and the crackling jagged night
lightening crazing the black rain soaked
sky, etching itself in an instant, then vanishing in rumbling
booms.
Fading into a still sun-soaked day
feeding the roots of collard
and pea, and bean, and tomato plants.
Sun from the sky.
Water from the earth
creates their tender growing.

And she in the silence
laboring over the Wall Street Journal
crossword, and
he reading Hemingway
remembering his own early days, in
Michigan.
Clear pebble-strewn trout streams,
tramping freely all day,
recreating now on the other end of life
newly minted freedoms
to do all day as you please,
while your parents smile at you from Heaven.

He's Gone

Past Lake Palestine again on a cloudy day
moving toward Austin I look for him.
Already, after seeing him twice, he has become a
fixture like a lover we have bedded
more than once.
Someone in my class told me he was dead,
had seen his body,
but I did not want to believe it, refusing the truth
just as we do when someone we love doesn't want us anymore.

Perhaps the buzzards
with their delicate and efficient functioning
have gotten him,
or the animal control people
who are paid to whisk death away.
At any rate, he is gone, my blue heron.

In Praise of Trees

They are there every day.
Everything else in our lives
moves,
is skittish.

The cats are unpredictable,
wander out beyond the fences
to encounter fierce dogs
with hot breath and eager barkings.

Lovers change
scintillate, show off
fresh facets of themselves,
which soothe the savagery of our need to control them.

And people die,
are born,
prance on stage,
stumble, run-off-
are carried off
by solemn & silent ushers
with carnations in their black lapels.

But the trees?
They remain,
caress our eyes every morning;
though the storms come
and strip them bare,
they just tuck themselves in,
dig deeper into the earth.

Making Love to the Body of the World

As we grow older, the urge
To see, to taste, to touch,
To be a sentient being in the world,
Grows more precious,
As if knowing our days
Are numbered,
Creates a hunger for simple experiences,
As a child encounters the world.

We ache to let go of all the mental
Constructions we have built
Over a lifetime,
Taking down all the ladders
We have placed against reality.

The hope of claiming
And understanding the meaning
Of it all, gives way to a
Gentleness, a desire
To simply be and know
All the contours of the world
As one travelling through it
Savoring the functioning of
Flesh
Making love to the body of the world.

Elegy for Montgomery Cowdry at Wilderways, Mount Selman, Texas

I.

Where is our lives?
Is it in the layers of
Artifacts: toy soldiers, boy
Scout badges, baseball cards,
The archeology of my life stored
In my shed?
And of course the manuscripts and
Journals, words, words, words.
To read what I wrote then, to revisit
What I felt then, seems irrelevant
amid the press of present concerns.
Strangest of all, there is
No change. Same issues, same concerns.
No growth, no maturity, only elaboration, and different
Circumstances.
So, where is our lives?
On paper?
In things?
Clearly our lives are not in the past,
because the present challenges our minds
With the Question:
What comes next?

II.

Where are the lives of Louis and Ottilia,
My parents?
In photographs of them, so young,
So vigorous, so full of dreams?
In things of theirs I still possess?
In memories in my mind,
A chaos of incidents prismed
By my youthful perception?
I never knew them as they knew themselves,
Only my version of them.
Where really are their lives?
I mean in their wholeness
As firm statements
As beings forged and hammered out
By their actions and attitudes.
Nowhere?

Everywhere?
In God?

Wherever their lives are now,
They probably are smiling at the concerns
of we who are
Earth bound, body bound.
Yet if we who are here, do not
Live our bodies, have those concerns
Why be here?
If life is not serious, relevant,
Why live it?

III.

I have been silent now for
Five days living among the
Things of my past often
On the verge of tears and some deep sadness.
My life is in
Some between time now
As is the earth, in early March,
Neither winter nor spring.
No force field drives it
No desire defines it.
It's a delicacy. A waiting. A listening.
A gathering.
To consolidate, to count,
To assess, enumerate, and the urge
to put everything I am into boxes, labeled.

IV.

Again I ask where is
My life?
I wish I could grasp it firmly in my teeth
And shake it awake,
As some giant terrier would.
But my teeth are also in limbo.
I'm waiting for two crowns.

V.

My time at this cabin
Is limited.
Montgomery, my landlord, grows more frail,

Is beginning his descent into
The body of earth he loves so deeply.
This thirty acres of untainted earth which he calls Wilderways.

VI.

He will go, peacefully
Some night, in his sleep,
No fuss, no pain.
"I'm gonna at least make my
Ninetieth birthday this June,"
He told me, "for bragging rights."

VII.

His daughters have now removed this giant of the earth
From the farm, taken him under their wings
Over somewhere by Austin,
To better care for him, they say.
But when his spirit does
Go on permanent pilgrimage from this body,
I know a cloud of smoke will
Rise from the chimney of his
Empty farmhouse and
Dissolve into an aching blue sky,
Etched against a golden sun rising in the east.

VIII.

Where is our lives?
Both nowhere and everywhere.
In the fierceness of the fire ants and wasps,
In the flash of the cardinals, and the fuss
Of the blue jays
Who play in the air of the yard.
Beginnings and Endings.
Spring times and Autumns,
Interwoven
In wild and weird ways.
Which are mostly unpredictable.

Coping With Change

A misty, foggy morning.
The world cradled in quiet,
I walk to the mailbox,
and a fat crow shatters
the morning silence with
his raucous cries.

I am here; I have a warm office,
feel the blood beat in
my body, can sense all these
things and am proud that I
began the day, after first
opening my eyes,
in silent prayer and meditation.

Yesterday, the need to get change for
a newspaper impelled me to
the Walmart Super Center
at an early hour and the sunrise
was breaking through a thick layer
of clouds in orange and red and pink
on display for any of us humans
who happen to be awake
to be up and alert to novelty
other than our usual thoughts
about sex, money, and achievement
or the lack thereof.

What do we have when we grow older?
What can we truly possess?
Money, I suppose.
Friends? perhaps, but they die
off and move away also.
Children? Not a chance -
they rattle about the world
on their own tracks and
at their own speed.
The poems we have written?
Yes, oh yes - they
will stay the same,
word after perfect word,
a monument to our speculations
whether anyone else cares or not.

As the Year Ends

Days fold gently into
the shortening
days of autumn.
It grows quiet as the
blanket of the year covers
the year's growing.

And the humans continue
to create dramatic events,
strut, rage, grieve, and, most of all
pretend that they are important
as the days fold gently
into the deepening darkening,

There are still green leaves
glinting in
raucous sunshine,
demanding our attention,
and yet the cool breeze,
the descending darkness easily
enfolds the clamor of each
Day, says, "rest, let go,
be not afraid.
Stoke fires."

Embrace the shortening days for even
In darkness there is life, curled up,
contained, serene.

At My Cabin

I draw small cabins to
myself.
I have lived in many of them
in a variety of places.
Their modesty frees us.
They claim little of our attention
and are easily maintained.

A large house with
many rooms
sucks our soul
and keeps us busy;
the ego itches to inhabit
all that space,
claim it for its own

On the other hand,
A small cabin
does not demand
but simply serves.

Deep In January

It's deep down into January,
pushing surely through the month.

One day is warm gold sun flowing
bathing us in promise
with reveries of camping
by crystal streams under blue skies,
with perfect companionship
and the next is grey,
with an angry leaf shredding machine,
marching across the grass,
grinding into tiny bits the last
evidence of Autumn.

Jane on the Telephone

Jane on the phone,
lines of communication always reaching
out like those squirrels she saw scratching
each other love play going after ticks.

Telephone talk late at night
words flitting across the coffee moist.
Saying
into the world are you there, knock knock.
Say there
are you there?

Bang, bang, let me scratch the tick
from my neck
before it sucks blood,
knowing all that stuff about
needing to find yourself
is so much dung shoveled
by a psychobabbler who never
talked with anyone late at night over a cup of coffee.

Unplanned Destination:
An Elegy for the Columbia

I.

An ordinary Saturday.
A blue Texas sky, and the sun shining.
A warm day on the way,
A reprieve from winter
When, suddenly, they fell from the sky.

This was no metaphor.

I was in my cabin, and with
The electric heater humming,
To take the chill off morning
A boom, and after-shock like thunder rolling,
took me away from newspaper and morning coffee
to the yard where I looked around and asked myself "Has Dallas been nuked?"

Later, talking with a friend,
I learned that, like Icarus, Columbia had
Fallen from the sky, and debris like
grisly rainfall,
was littering the East Texas landscape.

But this was no myth.

And so, exactly one hundred years, after the
first bumbling awkward lift off
from Kitty Hawk where the Wright Brothers,
Shade tree mechanics and inventors
Launched us upward for twelve seconds,
and after we reached the moon, planted human feet
on that spinning wasteland, this....
this... this what? Accident? Tragedy?

How quickly life can be snuffed out,
The body shucked off, one minute alive and
Full of physical intent, and in an instant
Hurled into the heavens, into Heaven.

And this is no metaphor.

And they, seven Icareans, who dared
The heavens, dared fate, themselves
With their craft, fell into the
Piney woods of East Texas and Louisiana,
fell with the vehicle they had
trusted and relied upon with their lives.

II.

On that first day of February, a clear day
With hints of springtime, the god of the Old Testament
was in charge.
Not the kindness of instant snuffing
out of the candles of their lives; not the decency of instant
cremation.
No mercy for them that day, that clear day
in February full of innocence and the promise of springtime.
Instead, the gross parts of bodies, wrenched from spirit, falling
to earth, littering the countryside, along
with metal and plastic.
The soaring spirits, the courageous hearts, the artful craft
which incarnated the best the mind of man
could do, reduced to these:
a helmet, a shoe, part of a wing:
What was once an incredible
Creation, the human body, and the body
Which carried it boldly ascending
 to the sun, is now debris:
Stuff, things, chunks, aftermath, chaos.

And body parts falling to earth,
are no metaphor.

III.

Those who learned of this event,
and especially we who live in East Texas,
who heard the thunder, who felt the shaking,
could also have been snuffed out, in an instant,
had a chunk of debris landed in the wrong place, at the wrong
time.

I, in my cabin, with coffee and newspaper,

Was spared once again as my mind drifts
Back to that time when I sat in the
Heart of downtown Detroit.
Four august Republican
Delegates were dining, sitting over supper
In the wide-open ground floor
of the atrium at the Renaissance Center,
when a sound like a shot startled our ruminations.
Someone from high above
had dropped a heavy glass which exploded into a
Thousand tiny fragments when it hit the floor next to us.
A three-foot difference, could have ended my
Life in an instant, or left me a drooling
Vegetable in a wheelchair,
A ward of the state of Michigan.
That glass was no metaphor.

And once again, on February first, the year two thousand and three,
my luck held. Nothing from the sky dropped on me.
I was out of the path of things falling from heaven.

IV.

Circumstance, Time, Space. Why these
Seven? Why now? Why not the next flight?
Ignorant preachers, and Muslim fanatics,
who noticed that the city of
Palestine was in the field of debris
Will perhaps draw some
Lesson about sin or hubris, as if God manages
each individual molecule of the
Universe, unable to face the
Real terror that perhaps the God of Chance,
Or Circumstance, or Chaos, the Watcher
over this Wasteland, has a say in things;
And that sometimes things just go
Wrong for no reason at the wrong time.

Humans hate the irrational,
regularly pretend it does not exist,
even though our lives are ruled by emotion and image,
and most of our choices are driven by myths written on our hearts.

There must be a reason.
There must be a reason.
There *must be* a *reason*. Musn't there?

Why did not, that huge chunk from the nose of Columbia
Crash through the roof of my cabin and
Launch me into heaven? Is there a
Reason? Did angels
Divert it, because God still has some use for me
In this body, on this earth, at this time, or
Did it just happen that way? Does someone
Win the lottery because God intends them to,
Or is it numbers, chance, chaos?

What is metaphor? What is reality? Who runs things?
Surely, someone does.

V.

And, in the end, what is there to say about this?
The human thirst to do what has not been
Done before, to see what has not been seen
Before, to risk our lives, to lay it all on the line in order
To know, fuels our race.
Will our benign and beneficent
Government, will our schools, our lawyers
our mothers, be able to breed this hunger out
Of the human race?
No, none of that will cease.
It is our craziness that often saves us.
If Paul Gaugin had stayed in Paris and grown
Rich and fat and faithful, would we be better off, or
Did he bless us all by running off to Tahiti?

Was it sane, of Charles Lindburg, to set off in
The spirit of St. Louis across the long and lonely
Miles of potential death on the way to Paris?
Why did he not stay home and sip
Martinis at poolside in Florida?
Would not this have been more sensible?

VI.

And what were they thinking,

What were the ruminations of our seven adventurous Icareans,
When they were twenty minutes from touchdown
In the tropics of Florida?
Shapes and curves, and the feel of one's feet on the
Ground; swimming in a pool; a glass or two, or three,
Or four, or five, or six, of wine; making slow
liesurely love with long langerous touches
of warm, human earth-bound flesh; a steak, ribeye,
slowly grilled over charcoal; the scent
and touch and taste of earth, dense and erotic.

It will take millennia and millennia and
Maybe a few more to make us into beings
who are all head with nothing below our navels.

Pure thought is perhaps our destiny,
But not yet, not yet.

VII.

Five score years ago, two bachelor brothers
Defied the pull of earth's gravity
With man-made power, launched an era,
A century which saw men walk on the moon,
Leave human footprints on that cold, black,
bleak place of dust and rock.

Our seven now are launched to an
Unplanned destination, the ultimate human
Unknown, where some claim to have gone,
And returned from, but nothing is really known with certainty.

The logic of Socrates still makes sense.
Death is either the portal to fresh
Individual opportunity
(Socrates survives).
Or nothingness, reversion to mental sleep,
the blank unremembering before our birth
(Socrates is gone).

Either of which is okay with him,
Because, should Socrates survive, he will have
stimulating discussions with the philosophers who
have preceded him into death, and should

Socrates cease to be, since there is no <u>he</u>
to experience the lack, there will be no loss.

VIII.

There is then, nothing really to grieve, nothing to say:
Having "broken the bonds of surly earth,"
lacking weight, density, space and time,
being soaring unfettered souls,
these brave seven, Husband, McCool, Clark, Chawla,
Brown, Anderson, and Ramon are indeed in a better place,
because these things, time, space, our bodies
limit the infinite lust of our hungry souls.

The physical shackles us to one tedious step at a time;
our fear of death prevents us from
living for the moment, and devouring all
the good, all the joy there is, without guilt,
without regret, and without shame.

Our seven Icareans, are either free spirits
Roaming a fresh new world, or are
Nothing, feel nothing, know no lack, and so, either way,
neither pity nor tears are needed by them, but rather
in our Brave New World of no risk,
our world which consumes us with lust for what we
lack, and fear for what we might lose, perhaps we need them.

An Elegy for Horace Edison

It was a two-day April downpour, coming in waves during the day and throughout the night, pattering across our roof, like thousands of tiny elfin feet, determined to soak the land.

Returning from a walk to the dam, we saw Horace standing, staring at the culvert, shaking his head at the trickle running through it, disturbed that the lake's safety valve was plugged up and ineffective.

"Ought to knock out that concrete," he said, "or water will flood across here and tear up half the yard; maybe break the dam."

Side by side, we took turns with the pry bar chipping concrete chunk by chunk, with the pent-up lake water spurting through, eager to be free. While I was taking a turn, heaving the heavy iron bar, he stood at the side of the culvert, taking a break.

I heard a thump, looked over and saw him lying in the ditch, face up. I jumped down to keep his face from the water, and started yelling for help. Willetta came, and Corene, and Howard and Joey and we did what we could for him, while the ambulance was on its way.

In terms of ways to leave this earth, there are worse ones. One moment Horace was fully alive, doing what he did: Giving himself for the good of the community of souls who live at Pinecrest Lake. The next, he was gone. No more cutting grass down by the lake, burning debris, or chasing coyotes away with his shotgun, so that all of our pets, could live in peace.

And who knows, perhaps he saved our lake, a last gesture in a life full of good deeds.

We all wish that he was still with us, wearing that old straw hat, working his garden, being a good neighbor. And when you think of it, is there a better way to go, instantly, out of doors, with your boots on, doing something useful?

An Ordinary Sunday Morning

Just an ordinary Sunday morning
in an ordinary neighborhood
in October
in America
with the sun slanting early
through the still green leaves
and a few blackbirds cawing
in early morning communication,
as the world
moves inexorably
toward the millennium.

Everyone around me in this neighborhood
has found food and shelter and is at least
seeking love-
Among my neighbors
I see no revolutions, dramas,
or insane cravings
that the world
conform to their image of it.

How precious, how priceless
how nourishing
this ordinary, the normal
which comes
dropping patiently into our lives
day after day.

The Eye of the Mockingbird

A blank look,
no fear
as I stare at him
that mockingbird on a branch
about five feet away from me,
through the glass of my windshield,
in the parking lot
of the Jacksonville public library.
"There is nothing more to
do today," I tell myself
as I sit and we stare at each other.
"I can do this, just sit and look at him."

No one knows he is
there now, no one cares.
That branch,
and the world is his
to travel as he wills,
to take any stance he chooses to make.
His mother
does not know where he is.
His mate does not know where he is.
But I know,
and he knows, where I am.

This knowing is our bond,
our perfect
and fulfilling aloneness in the world.

Alone

A school bus. Autumn. Crisp air.
The coolness of summer vanished
when heat wrapped itself around
you like some omnipresent
lover sticking to your every pore and crease.

Things are sharper now. Edges clearer.
You can see vast distances and make leaps of
faith bounding over hills
which you have not yet seen,
and almost laugh
because we are either immortal or not.

And those trees snaking up out of the earth
in their tangled glory,
are not a question mark,
but an answer;
stripped now, in autumn,
they too know God, exist,
and are making children merrily.

Peter Hoheisel has published poems in national publications, such as *The Nation*, and many regional ones, a few of which are the *Langdon Review*, *Grasslands Review*, *Nebo*, and *Iconoclast*. As well as teaching Creative Writing, Literature and Composition, at Lon Morris College in Jacksonville, Texas, he was also chair of the department of Religion and Philosophy at that institution. Before he moved to Texas, he was awarded numerous grants to teach poetry in many schools through the Michigan Council for the Arts and in Tyler, Texas, under a grant from the Texas Commission for the Arts.